T0130043

SHAGGY DOGS ARE PUNNY TALES

Gene Child

Illustrations by
Gene Youngmann

A pair of Genes

2nd Edition

iUniverse, Inc.
Bloomington

SHAGGY DOGS ARE PUNNY TALES

iUniverse books may be ordered through booksellers or by contacting:

iUniverse
1663 Liberty Drive
Bloomington, IN 47403
www.iuniverse.com
1-800-Authors (1-800-288-4677)

Because of the dynamic nature of the Internet, any web addresses or links contained in this book may have changed since publication and may no longer be valid. The views expressed in this work are solely those of the author and do not necessarily reflect the views of the publisher, and the publisher hereby disclaims any responsibility for them.

Any people depicted in stock imagery provided by Thinkstock are models, and such images are being used for illustrative purposes only.

Certain stock imagery © Thinkstock.

ISBN: 978-1-4759-9123-9 (sc)
ISBN: 978-1-4759-9124-6 (e)

Library of Congress Control Number: 2013908954

Printed in the United States of America.

iUniverse rev. date: 5/28/2013

DEDICATION

To Arlone, my wife, whose tolerance and patience while listening to these stories over and over through the years was above and beyond the call of duty . . . and matrimony.

Also, to all those students who left my physics classes bewildered.

Table of Contents

FOREWORD

Belly-laughers should beware: this book could be hazardous to the health of your sense of humor. It is an unauthorized collection of outrageous dog-wagging tales with no socially redeeming qualities, no purpose except to provoke laughter and leave readers with the hang-dog look that comes from being taken in by a snake-oil salesman.

On the other hand, as Tevye was wont to say, these curly canine anecdotes will banish blues, cure choler, delete depression and make all who read them healthier, wealthier and wiser.

Robert Tweedell, retired journalist, *The Denver Post*

INTRODUCTION

There was usually a ripple of laughter in the classroom, ranging from tentative chuckles to appreciative belly-laughs. There were also groans here and there, and a few blank faces. Whatever the ultimate reaction, it was generally preceded by a moment or two of silence, during which minds were racing in a search for the humor of the story. It must have been funny! Some people were laughing.

The punch line, preferably involving a pun, is the culmination of an often labored, embellished tale that in our oral literature has been labeled a "shaggy dog" story. Its preservation and continuation is an ongoing saga to which you may all contribute. All you need do is imaginatively construct an elaborate tale leading to a punch line, often a play on words or a pun that will take the listener completely off guard.

I started telling these stories to students in my physics classes years ago. Eventually it became traditional for me to wind up each week's series of classes with a story. Many came from the students themselves, others I picked up from friends and colleagues, and some I invented. The humor may be sophomoric, but it tickled the funny bones of high school juniors and seniors, many of their parents, and others who had a well developed sense of humor.

It is more fun to tell a "shaggy dog" than to hear one. I savor the response of the listener, especially the unsuspecting one exposed for the first time to one of the stories; the rewards of raconteurs are great.

The stories can be adapted to suit the audience; they can be told straightforwardly, without elaborations, and with just a trace of a pause before the punch-line is delivered. They can also be drawn out almost interminably. It is much better to draw them out. Enhance them with as much detail as you can muster, keeping the listener off balance and teetering in anticipation of the delayed denouement.

Telling a "shaggy dog" story is really an exercise in oral dexterity. With practice, you will find the exercise pure delight. Don't just read these stories and groan. Try them out with any embellishments or adaptations you can devise that seem appropriate for your audience of the moment, and ENJOY!

The last story of the book, The Race Horses, is typical of the type most people first think of when they recognize that they have been trapped into a situation in which they may have to listen to a "shaggy dog" story. It is a long and complicated story that seems to drag on forever. The punch line is so inane most listeners wonder why they didn't excuse themselves halfway through the story. You wonder what sadistic joy the teller of the tale could possibly derive by relating all the details. You needn't read the last story unless you have masochistic tendencies.

Clichés

The Original Shaggy Dog Story

B ack in the middle Ages, before we had shaggy dog stories, if you can imagine such a terrible state of affairs, there was a young midget who wanted desperately to be a knight. He didn't want to be just any knight. He wanted to be a knight of King Arthur's Round Table. His friends laughed when he told them of his secret desire. In spite of the ridicule, he persisted and managed to gain an audience with King Arthur.

After hearing his request, King Arthur said, "You couldn't even mount a horse, let alone kill a dragon or rescue a damsel in distress."

The midget replied, "Yes I can, just let me try!"

"Well, I guess it won't hurt to give you a chance," King Arthur admitted. "If you can rescue a damsel in distress or kill a dragon, I will make you a knight."

The midget, of course, had a plan. He needed a big dog. He searched high and low until he found just the right dog, a great big shaggy St. Bernard which was just the right size for him to ride.

He took the dog to the local cobbler. "Can you make me a saddle so I can ride this dog?" he asked.

The cobbler chuckled and said, "Sure, compared to the full sized saddles I usually make that will be easy."

Next the midget went to the local blacksmith. "Do you have any plowshares you could make into a sword and a suit of armor for me?" he asked.

The blacksmith replied, "Certainly. You are so small only one ploughshare would do the trick." The blacksmith measured him carefully and told him to return

a week later. When the midget
returned, the armor fit perfectly
and the sword in its scabbard was
sharp as a razor.

Early the next morning, the
midget saddled up his big shaggy
dog and rode off into the deep,
dark forest looking for either a
damsel in distress or a dragon to
slay. He rode and rode and rode
all day, but found neither damsel
nor dragon. By late afternoon he
was really discouraged. He became
frightened when he heard thunder
in the distance and saw a huge rain
cloud rapidly approaching. He
knew if it rained on his new suit
of armor it would rust so that he
would never get it off.

He whipped the shaggy dog
into a gallop and began searching
for shelter. Eventually, he saw a little
thatched hut ahead in a clearing.
He rode the dog into the clearing,
reined him to a halt, jumped to
the ground, and clattered up to the
door. He pounded on the door with
all his might. A little shriveled-up
lady came to the door, opened it
just a crack, and exclaimed:

"What's a knight like you doing out on a

dog like this?"

Bank Robbers

The financial situation had been very bad for months. Because he was out of work and destitute, a young man decided to rob a bank. After days of surveillance, he chose a small satellite bank facility across the metropolitan area from where he was living. He spent several days planning every move. Late one dark moonless night he picked the lock on the rear door of the bank without difficulty. He stealthily crept through the bank to the place where he knew the safe stood.

Then his troubles began. While trying to pick the lock on the safe, he set off the burglar alarm but his careful preparation paid off. He had brought along a furniture dolly so quickly loaded the small safe onto the dolly and rolled it out to his van.

He drove to his friend's house and explained his problem. He asked if, in exchange for some of the loot, he might store the safe in the garage for a few days.

The friend assured him:

You can rest assured, your safe is secret with me!

The Philandering Czechoslovakian

During the early 60s a young Czechoslovakian man escaped to the west. After a few years, he settled in New York. He was quite a man with the women and, as a result, had some narrow escapes. Once, when he was in the apartment of a married lady, the husband unexpectedly returned. She said he wouldn't fit under the bed and the husband was sure to hang his clothes in the closet. The only thing to do was to crawl out on the ledge outside the window.

"But it's the tenth floor!" he exclaimed.

She convinced him she could quickly get rid of her husband, so out onto the ledge he climbed. The scantily clad Czech shivered on the ledge for minute after minute while the husband changed clothes and made himself comfortable. It soon became apparent he was home for the evening.

Finally, the Czech became desperate and crawled along the ledge to the next apartment. The lady in the bedroom there was startled out of her wits when he tapped on the window. He was eventually able to convince her to raise the window just a crack so he could whisper:

"You wouldn't be able to cache a Czech would you?"

Immortal Porpoises

A rich California man decided to improve his health by taking up swimming. He built an Olympic-sized swimming pool so he could swim every day. After a few years he tired of the routine so the pool was left unused for months at a time.

Eventually, the man became fascinated with bird watching. He decided to build an aviary over the pool so he wouldn't have to go out into the woods to bird watch. He ended up with a huge netted canopy that covered his entire backyard. He collected many varieties of birds, both rare and common. Later, he decided to collect rare and unusual fish to be placed in his unused pool. He bought more and bigger fish until eventually he bought two porpoises.

Years went by. The porpoises got old and lethargic. He didn't know what to do with them. One day, when out observing his collection of creatures, he noticed that the mynah birds were dive bombing the porpoises. As he watched, a porpoise leaped out of the water and caught a mynah in his mouth.

Over a period of time the mynah birds became fewer and fewer. But the man noticed a change in the porpoises. They began to cavort around like they had when they were young.

He thought, "I've discovered the fountain of youth for porpoises- mynah birds."

He went to the local pet shop to re-supply his aviary with mynah birds. As he was driving back from the pet shop, he heard on the radio that two lions had escaped from the nearby state zoo.

When he arrived home, there on his front porch were the two escaped lions. He waited in his car watching them. When they hadn't moved after an hour or so, he became concerned about his beloved porpoises. Screwing up his courage, he got out of the car, ran up to the porch, jumped across the lions, went through the house and released the mynahs above the pool. A short time later, there was a knock on the front door. Two policemen stood there.

The man asked, "What's the problem?"

One of the policemen replied, "We've come to arrest you. You have been charged with:

Transporting mynahs across state lions for

immortal porpoises."

Young Gulls

Many of you may not be aware that the Kansas City zoo is shared by Kansas City, Kansas and Kansas City, Missouri. A part of the zoo is on each side of the state line. All the fish are on the Missouri side and the birds are on the Kansas side.

Several years ago, attendance was falling at the aquarium so it was decided to start a marine show like the one at Sea World in San Diego. Their aquarium personnel were able to train the porpoises to do all the usual tricks; jumping over barriers, throwing balls into the air and so forth. Attendance quickly increased. One day a problem arose; the porpoises began to do sexually explicit acts during the show.

The zoo director called a meeting of the aquarium personnel. A trainer suggested, "Let's do something to distract the porpoises, like feeding them something extra during the show. What do porpoises eat besides fish?"

"I've noticed they sometimes eat small sea gulls," another trainer answered.

"That's it! I'm sure we can get fledgling sea gulls from the aviary," the first trainer said.

The director of the bird house confirmed that there was a surplus of young sea gulls. Before the next porpoise show, one of the trainers went over to the bird house where he filled a container with fledgling gulls and headed back for the aquarium. As he crossed the line dividing Kansas from Missouri he was stopped by the highway patrol and was arrested. The charge was:

Transporting young gulls across the state line for immoral porpoises!

Bear Hunting

Three hunters, a Pole, a Czech, and a Hungarian, went bear hunting. When they didn't return on schedule, their wives called the authorities, who sent out a search party.

The searchers found the hunters' camp all torn apart. There were bear tracks everywhere. The embers of the fire were scattered! The tent was torn to shreds and the men's rifles were nowhere to be found. The searchers followed the bear tracks through the woods until they found three bears, a male and his mate with a young cub nearby. They shot the female and found the remains of the Pole and Hungarian in her stomach but the male and the cub escaped.

No sign of the missing hunter could be found. The search party reached the only obvious conclusion:

The Czech was

in the male.

The Circus Bassett Hound

Once there was a circus that was, without a doubt, the best circus in the world because it boasted the best lion tamer in the world. He was spectacular! The lions would do whatever he said. The high point of the lion show was, of course, when he would stick his head in a lion's mouth! When the circus started losing money the owner started selling off animals and equipment to help meet expenses. He called the Lion Tamer into his office.

"I'd really like to keep you on, because you and your lions are the star of the show", the owner said, "But I've had to sell your lions because they cost too much to feed. Still, you're good, and we need you, so if you can come up with an act with what we have left, we'll keep you on."

"Well, I do need a job," the Lion Tamer replied, "What animals do we have left?"

"To tell you the truth," the owner said, "the only animal I have left is my faithful old Bassett hound. I'd never sell him!"

"He'll do," said the Tamer.

So the Lion Tamer worked with the Bassett hound and taught him the entire lion act. The dog caught on right away, but there was a problem. There was no way the Lion Tamer's head was going to fit into the dog's mouth.

"My foot will fit," the Lion Tamer said, so he tried it, and sure enough the dog picked that up too.

Opening night, the Lion Tamer did the act with the Bassett hound, and the crowd loved it. They'd never seen anything like it before. At the end of the act, when the Lion Tamer put his foot into the dog's mouth, the crowd went wild.

"Encore, encore!" the crowd yelled.

Well, the Lion Tamer hadn't thought of an encore before, so he thought to himself, "If one foot is good, two is better."

So he stuck his other foot into the dog's mouth! Well, the two feet together are almost as big as 4the dog's head, so the dog was choking and gasping, and finally out of self-preservation, he clamped his jaws shut, biting off the Lion Tamer's legs at the ankles.

And the moral of this story?

Don't put all your legs in one Bassett!

Quasimodo

Quasimodo, the hunch back, lost his arms in a terrible accident. He was out of work for months. He was short of money, so he was desperate. One day, while looking through a Paris newspaper help-wanted section, he noticed that Notre Dame Cathedral was advertising for part-time help.

He went in for an interview with one of the priests. Fortunately the priest on duty didn't know Quasimodo.

The new priest explained they were looking for a bell ringer and said, "I'm very sorry, but obviously you couldn't do the job without arms."

Quasimodo replied, "Just try me. Take me up to the bell tower and I'll show you." They climbed the 195 steps to the top of the bell tower.

The priest asked, "How do you expect to ring the bell?"

Quasimodo took a position directly in front of the bell, drew back at the waist, and bending forward rapidly, struck the bell with his forehead as hard as he could.

The priest said, "No, no, that will never do. It was not loud enough."

Quasimodo said, "I can do better than that. Let me show you."

He retreated to the far side of the bell tower, ran as fast as he could, dived head first at the bell, but missed. He flew out the window, and fell 140 feet to the street below.

The priest rushed down the stairs to the street. By the time he got there a crowd had clustered around Quasimodo.

As he pushed his way through, someone in the crowd said, "Father, Father, who is this? Do you know him?"

The priest said, "No, I don't, but;

His face sure

rings a bell!"

Moromodo

Quasimodo, the hunchback of Notre Dame, had a nephew whose name was Moromodo. Like his uncle, Moromodo had lost both arms at the elbows. No one would hire a cripple during those times so he became destitute. Then he heard about a part-time job at Notre Dame Cathedral. He went to the church for an interview with the new priest.

"You can't pull the bell rope with those stubs of yours," the priest said.

Moromodo replied, "Yes I can. Just take me up to the top of the bell tower and I'll show you I can ring the bell."

The priest was reluctant but finally agreed to take Moromodo up the 195 steps to the top of the tower. Moromodo stood in front of the bell, then banged it with his forehead as hard as he could.

The priest said, "That will never do. That's not loud enough."

Moromodo replied, "I can ring it louder than that. Let me show you." He walked back to the other side of the bell tower, turned and ran as fast as he could at the bell. He leaped at the bell, missed and flew out the window to the street 140 feet below.

The priest rushed down the stairs. A crowd had gathered around the fallen Moromodo.

As he pushed his way through the crowd someone asked, "Father, Father, is it Quasimodo again?"

The priest replied:

"No, but it sure is a dead ringer, isn't it?"

The Head

Many years ago a man walked into a bar carrying a human head under his arm. He walked up to the bar, sat down and placed the head on the counter beside him. He ordered two beers. When the bartender brought the beers, the man drank one and carefully held the glass for the head to drink the second. No sooner had the head finished the beer than it grew a torso.

The man ordered two more beers, drank one and held the other for the head and torso to drink. Shortly, the body grew arms. The man ordered two more beers, gave one to his friend and drank the other. The head-torso-arms grew legs. Then the new "body" ordered two beers. Soon after the beers were gone, "poof", the new body, head, torso, legs and arms, disappeared.

This just goes to show again:

You should quit while you're a head!

The Midget Medium

As with many short people, Fred, a midget, was very conscious of his size. He was very sensitive because of all the teasing he had been subjected to through the years. Fred had trouble finding an occupation that fit his abilities. But he had been blessed with a wonderful talent; he could foretell the future.

To take advantage of his ability, he became a medium. He set up an office, bought some billboard space along the main thoroughfare in town and advertised in the local paper. Business was not what he expected and he soon found that there was not a lot of money in fortune telling. He began looking for some other way to earn a living.

He went into crime as a burglar. Being small, he found he could slip into some of the most unlikely places. He could climb up the side of a building, squeeze through a window, gather up the valuables in an apartment and be gone without leaving a trace.

However, as you all know, crime doesn't pay! Eventually, he was arrested, taken to trial, convicted and sent to prison. Again, being a very small, he found that he could slip between the iron bars that guarded the windows of his cell so late one night he escaped.

The newspaper headlines the next day proclaimed:

"*Short Medium at large!*"

The Moose Hunter

My brother, David, who lives in Maine, tells this story. Several years ago he owned a roan stallion he had trained to hunt moose. His stallion could smell moose at least a mile away. Most, who have been near enough to notice, agree that moose do have a distinctive odor.

When moose season arrived David would saddle up the roan and ride off into the woods. He would simply allow the horse to wander aimlessly, and almost invariably they would find moose the first day of the season. The horse was able to approach a moose without frightening it, so that Dave could easily bag it with a single shot.

This horse became famous all over Maine for its extraordinary ability. Dave was the envy of hunters from one end of Maine to the other because his family was assured an ample supply of moose mince meat every Christmas.

One fall day, when Dave went out to feed the horse, he found it had been stolen. He spread the word about his loss, but moose season came and went without the return of his roan stallion.

Shortly after moose season closed, a pickup truck drove into Dave's farmyard with the missing horse in a trailer.

The driver said, "I'm bringing your horse back because he's no good. We didn't find any moose all season!"

My brother replied, " I could have told you:

A stolen roan

gathers no moose!"

The Shan

The ruler of one of the small Middle Eastern kingdoms is referred to as a "Shan," not a king. Many years ago the reigning Shan was prone to epileptic fits. Because of the condition of the Shan, the prime minister rarely left the country. He felt he always had to be nearby in order to protect the Shan.

Once, however, it became necessary for the prime minister to be absent from the kingdom for several days. When he returned to the capital city, he found destruction everywhere. Bodies were lying about, windows and doors were broken and trash was strewn all over the streets.

The prime minister rushed to the palace where he found one man who wasn't quite dead.

He lifted the man's head and asked, "What happened?

The man replied:

"*Where were you when the fit hit the Shan?*"

The Stage

A young man had just received a new Corvette as an early high school graduation gift. One night he was out driving around showing off the car, but found that most of his friends were in the high school auditorium practicing for the senior play. He spent most of the evening roaring around the streets in front of the school awaiting the end of the rehearsal.

During one pass of the school, he lost control of the car and crashed through the rear wall of the auditorium. The car finally came to a stop right on the middle of the stage. Fortunately, no one was hurt.

Several of the aspiring young actors rushed up to the demolished car. As they pulled their dazed friend out of the wreckage, he muttered:

"Pardon me, this is just a stage I'm going through."

Nate the Snake

Once upon a time in the desert southwest there was a prospector who had been in the hills alone for months. He was lonely and needed supplies, so he headed for town with his donkey. While moseying along a dusty trail, the prospector heard a voice.

"Hi, stop a minute. I'd like to talk to you." The prospector looked around, saw nothing so started on down the trail.

"Hey, wait a minute. Don't you want to talk?" asked the voice. The prospector stopped again and carefully looked all around. He saw nothing except a small green snake curled up on a large rock beside the trail. He knew snakes couldn't talk so he started off again.

The voice called, "Hey, don't go! I'm Nate, the talking snake. I just love to talk to people. Won't you stay to talk?"

The prospector could hardly believe his ears, but was lonely and curious, so he turned back and sat on a rock near Nate. They talked for hours. Nate knew all about gold prospecting, mining, and was even informed about world events. An idea occurred to the old prospector.

He said, "You know, Nate, I bet there are lots of people who would just love to talk with you. Let's form a partnership. I'll go down into town and buy a tent. We'll set up the tent right here beside this trail and charge people a pokey of gold to talk with you. We'll split the take 50-50."

Nate replied, "I don't have much use for money, but I just love to talk to people. It's a deal!"

The prospector was back in two days with a tent, a supply of grub and the materials they would need to make some signs. He had spread the word while in town and soon people were coming long distances to hear this talking snake. Over the next few months, the word spread far and wide.

People went out of their way to stop for a chat with Nate. The snake became so well known that when wagon trains headed west many followed the trail that led past Nate's tent. Many wagon masters planned their trips so they could circle the wagons around Nate's tent at least one night. Nate just loved all the attention.

The old prospector grew rich, the trail became a paved road, and a log cabin was built where Nate could live. In due time the old prospector died, but Nate seemed to go on forever. He just went on and on, talking to anyone who would listen.

Eventually, a town grew up around Nate's cabin. The town fathers realized that Nate was their star tourist attraction, so they built a large building where he could hold his audiences.

As fate would have it, when World War I came along, the U.S. government decided to build a munitions factory in the desert near Nate's town. The town grew and prospered but after the war disaster struck. The factory was closed. The town would have disappeared except for Nate and all the tourists he attracted.

During World War II, the munitions factory reopened and the town again prospered. After the war, when nuclear missiles were being developed, the munitions factory was converted into a nuclear missile factory. The most dangerous missile the world had ever seen was built in that factory. It was housed in a silo buried deep underground. The missile was so dangerous that if it were ever fired, the whole world would be blown up.

With a missile that dangerous you don't have the lever to fire it housed just anywhere. You put the lever in a place where it will be secure. The lever was protected in a blockhouse encircled with a high chain link fence. As chance would have it, the blockhouse had been built right across the road from Nate's house.

Late one night, Nate decided he wanted to see his girlfriend. She lived across the road near the blockhouse, so Nate went out for a slither. As he slithered across the road, there was a terrible accident! Nate was hit and killed by a car.

The town fathers were terribly upset at losing their prime tourist attraction so they mounted a major investigation. The driver of the car was brought in for questioning. He was placed under the hot lights and mercilessly interrogated. After hours of questioning, he broke down and confessed.

He admitted, "I was driving along and saw this little green snake in the road. I recognized Nate. I swerved, but saw that I would crash into the blockhouse containing the lever if I continued in that direction! I swerved back and hit Nate because I decided:

Better Nate

than lever!

You Can't Beat Beets

P ete the plumber took up gardening as a hobby. He grew all the usual vegetables such as lettuce, tomatoes and beans, but after several seasons, he became fascinated with beets.

He came to think, "You can't beat beets!"

One year, late in the season, he noticed that some of his beets were wilting. He called the local county extension agent for advice. After listening to Pete's description of the problem, the agronomist on duty decided he needed to personally look over the situation. They could not agree on a time when both could meet in the garden, so Pete gave the agronomist the address and a description of the house.

When the extension agent drove out to examine the beets, he forgot to take the address of Pete's house. He thought he remembered the address, but, when he arrived in the area, he found that two houses on the block fit the description, one with an even number and the other odd. Both had gardens with lots of beets. He queried a neighbor and learned that both houses belonged to plumbers. He chose to examine the beets in the garden that seemed most wilted.

Taking out his stethoscope, he carefully examined the beets. He quickly identified the problem, so returned to his office. Later, when Pete the plumber called, the agent learned he had been at the wrong address.

He exclaimed:

"My gosh, I've been listening to the beets of a different plumber!"

Eskimo Kayak

An Eskimo in Alaska was out fishing in his kayak when a violent storm overtook him. He wrapped up in his walrus robe as best he could, but soon realized he was going to freeze unless he did something quickly.

In desperation, he tore some of the ribs out of his kayak and built a small fire in the bottom of the boat to warm himself.

Of course, as you might imagine, the fire burned a hole in the bottom of the kayak. It sank and the Eskimo drowned.

This once again proves:

You can't have your kayak

and heat it, too!

Puns

The Indian Wire

There was once an Indian chief upon whose reservation oil was discovered. In an attempt to spend the newfound tribal wealth wisely, he decided to send his oldest son off to a private school. The son attended one of the best prep schools in the nation. He did well enough there to earn a scholarship to the Massachusetts Institute of Technology.

After four years of intense study the young Indian received a degree in electrical engineering and returned home to the reservation.

The proud chief arranged a tribal festival in honor of his son, the college graduate. The entire tribe celebrated for several days.

Near the end of the festivities, the son turned to his father and said, "I really do appreciate all you have done for me. I'd like to do something in return. Father, what can I do?"

The chief thought for a time, then said, "I have always wanted heat and an electric light in my outdoor toilet."

"I can do that with no trouble at all," said the grateful son.

The next day he went to town where he bought 10 miles of wire, some switches, plugs, sockets and the other things he needed. As soon as he returned, he installed an electric light in the outdoor toilet, thus becoming forever famous as:

The first Indian to wire a head for a reservation!

Blondes

A group of very attractive young female city employees discovered they could nicely supplement their incomes by moonlighting as call girls. After having her hair bleached one of the girls discovered she was more successful as a blonde. She convinced the others that the old saying, "Blondes have more fun," is true.

The ladies became so popular that they were able to charge exorbitant rates. They even charged their taxi fares to the Johns they served.

When hard times hit and the market got soft, they needed a bigger come-on. Some of them understood the economic law of supply and demand, so decided to lower their rates. One of the ways they used to lower their rates was to stop including their taxi fares in the fees they charged their customers.

They have become known as:

The taxi-free

municipal blondes.

Swen and Ollie

S wen was 50 years old, so Ollie arranged that they go out to dinner at a nice up-scale restaurant. During their meal, the lady at the next table choked on a bite of food. She clutched her throat, obviously having difficulty breathing. She rose to her feet, still clutching her throat, and staggered toward the table where Swen and Ollie were seated.

Swen very calmly got up from his chair, strode quickly over to a position behind the lady, lifted her skirt and pulled down her panties. He knelt down and began licking her on the behind.

This remarkable action startled the struggling woman. She stumbled forward and fell, striking the edge of the table. The food was dislodged from her throat and she was saved.

After the excitement had passed, Swen was finally able to sit again with Ollie.

She said, "Swen, you are such a wonderful man. You always know just what to do."

Swen replied, "Yes Ollie, that:

heinie lick maneuver always seems to work!"

Bar String

A string went into a bar to have a drink. As he walked in, the bartender carefully surveyed him. The string marched up to the bar and said, "Give me a shot of whiskey on the rocks."

The bartender asked, "Are you a string?" The string replied, "Certainly, I'm a string. Why do you ask?" "We don't serve strings in here, buddy!" the bartender growled. "OK, if that's your attitude, I'll take my business elsewhere," the string said and he slipped out the door.

He tried a couple of other bars and got the same treatment. As he was preparing to enter a fourth bar, the string tripped and tied himself in knots. He looked terrible. His top was in disarray. He straightened himself out as best he could, then resolutely strode into the first bar again.

When he ordered, the bartender said, "Are you a string?"

The string replied:

"No, I'm a

frayed knot."

Boo Bear

B oo Bear went into the bar to get a beer.

The bartender said, "We don't sell beer to bears in this bar, buddy."

Boo Bear replied, "I've just got to have a beer, sir!"

The bartender said, "No beers for bears in this bar buddy."

Boo Bear said, "If you don't give me a beer, bartender, I'm going right down to the end of the bar and eat that lady sitting there!"

The bartender would not give in.

He said again, "No beers for bears in this bar buddy!"

Boo Bear strode down to the end of the bar and attacked the lady. It was a terrible thing to watch. There wasn't even a hank of hair left when he finished.

He then returned to where the bartender had been watching and said very gruffly, "Now I want a beer!"

The bartender said, "We don't serve drug addicts in this bar buddy!"

Boo Bear asked, "What? What do you mean?"

The bartender pointed to the vacant stool and said:

"That was the bar bitch you ate, buddy!"

The Potato's Daughters

A potato had three daughters of marriageable age. The eldest daughter came to her father with an Irish potato in tow.

The father questioned the young potato carefully, then said, "Irish potatoes are of good stock. I give my blessing to this marriage! Go raise many little potatoes, my children."

The second daughter appeared with an Idaho potato. Again the father carefully questioned the prospective suitor.

He then decreed, "Idaho potatoes are of vigorous stock. You have my blessing for this marriage."

The third daughter later appeared before the father accompanied by the famous TV news anchorman, Brian Williams.

The old potato immediately went into a rage denouncing the proposed marriage.

He proclaimed vigorously to Mr. Williams:

"You're only a commentator!"

Impressionist Thief

A thief in Paris made elaborate plans to steal some paintings from the Louvre Art Museum. In particular he was interested in Impressionists paintings. He spent weeks studying the entrances and exits of the museum. He studied the alarm system in minute detail and learned how to disable it. He carefully observed the behavior of the guards to establish the pattern they took in making their rounds.

Late one night he put all his research into action. He was successful in penetrating all the security devices and carried 6 paintings out to his van.

He drove only about 2 blocks before he ran out of gas. Of course, the police caught and arrested him. During the interrogation that followed they asked why, with such an elaborate setup, he hadn't filled his van with gas.

His reply:

"I didn't have the Monet to buy Degas to make the Van Gogh!"

Focus Ranch
(A triple play)

A rich Texas oil man was growing old. He had three spoiled sons who spent money like the oil from whence it had come. The father was concerned that the fortune he had worked so hard to accumulate would be squandered by his prodigal sons.

After consultation with his lawyer, he decided to buy a ranch and set up the boys in the cattle business in order to force them to focus their energies on one huge project. He bought a 50,000 acre ranch and 5,000 head of cattle. Then he called his sons together to show them their inheritance.

"What should we name the ranch?" the sons asked.

The old man replied:

"The Focus Ranch: where the sons raise meat."

(sun's rays meet.)

Rudolph

Several years ago President George W. Bush and his wife Laura were meeting in Moscow with a group of Russian leaders, one of whom was named Rudolph Georsky. During a break in the talks, they noticed storm clouds gathering in the distance.

George turned to Laura and said, "Look, dear, it's going to snow."

"Nyet!" Rudolph exclaimed. "I've lived here all my life and I think it's not going to snow. It's going to rain!"

"Well," Bush responded, "It sure seems to be cold enough to snow."

Rudolph disagreed again and the argument became heated. Seeing no end to the argument, Laura interrupted and said to George:

"Rudolph, the red,

knows rain, dear!"

Mama Sparrow

Mama sparrow was sitting in the nest waiting for her eggs to hatch. There were four eggs in the nest on which she was sitting. Three were white but one was strangely different. It was speckled.

"Why is that one speckled?" asked Papa Sparrow.

Mama sparrow replied:

"I just did it for a Lark!"

The Obscene Son

Alan B. Cranston was a rich industrialist. His whole life had been devoted to making money. He had been so consumed by his business interests that he had never developed an interest in any hobbies, not even the ladies. As a result, he reached middle age with no wife and no children. Then, as he entered his declining years, he suddenly recognized there was no one to inherit the millions he had worked so hard to acquire.

Cranston decided he wanted an heir, but still had no use for women. He went to his doctor to explain the problem.

"I understand you can now clone human cells to make a new human being. Is that true?" he asked.

The doctor replied, "Yes, we have had some success with that procedure, but it's very expensive, you know."

"Money is no problem. I want a son!" said the industrialist. "I'll pay you whatever is necessary."

The doctor took some of Cranston's cells, treated them, and was successful in cloning a son, the spitting image of his father. The baby had the same nose, eyes, hair, everything.

Cranston hired nursemaids to raise the son and made sure he had the best of care. When the time came, he sent the boy to the best preparatory schools, then to the Harvard School of Business. When the son graduated from Harvard, his father welcomed him into the business as an equal partner. There was only one problem. The kid had a filthy mouth. Every third word was an obscenity. He just couldn't put together a complete sentence without at least one obscene word.

The father thought to himself, "He'll outgrow that."

The son didn't improve. He got worse. Business began to suffer because the son's obscene language was driving away prospective customers. The industrialist decided he had to do something quickly or face disaster.

After some thought, he decided that since his son was simply a clone he could do anything to him he wished. One day father and son went for a drive. They drove to the top of a nearby mountain, parked near a high cliff and got out of the car to enjoy the view. Seizing his opportunity, the father pushed his son over the edge of the cliff!

Cranston thought he had solved his problem, but someone had observed the dirty deed. The witness called the police and Cranston was arrested. He was charged with:

making an obscene clone fall!

Datsun Rain

A man who lived in a rural mid-western area had owned his Datsun truck for nearly 20 years. His deteriorating truck had become one of his prized possessions. Parts had become unavailable, even in the junk yards of Chicago.

When some of the cogs on the transmission gear of the truck were damaged, the local Datsun dealer found the only source of replacement cogs was to order directly from Japan. Since the farmer was eager to drive his truck as soon as possible, the cogs were shipped by air freight.

While flying over Iowa, the plane ran into a thunderstorm. The rear door flew open and out dropped the box of cogs. A local farmer, who saw them falling into one of his fields, turned to his wife and said:

"Look dear, it's

raining Datsun Cogs!

The Terns

Late one night, a Boeing DC-9 airplane crashed on the outskirts of Pueblo, Colorado. When the authorities investigated, they found the crew had disappeared, perhaps because the plane was loaded with three tons of marijuana.

Well, what do you do with three tons of marijuana? The officers rented a nearby warehouse in which to store the "grass" while they determined how to dispose of it. They finally decided that the marijuana would have to be burned. Of course, you can't just burn that much "grass" in the vicinity of a populated area. The entire population might end up high-as-a-kite if the wind blew from the wrong direction.

After weeks of searching, an abandoned incinerator was found in the nearby San Luis Valley. Plans were made to transport the marijuana to the site, but, as so often happens, a group of environmentalists heard of the project and objected. They were aware that a rare breed of tern nested along the shores of a lake just south of the incinerator site. There was concern that the smoke from burning three tons of marijuana might disturb the terns.

An injunction was issued to stop the proposed burn. The usual court proceedings dragged on for months before the environmentalists lost the case.

A few days later, the marijuana was taken to the incinerator site and all the necessary preparations for the big burn were completed. The same morning the "grass" was burned, the terns took to the wing to migrate north.

The terns flew directly over the incinerator and, as you might guess:

There wasn't a tern left unstoned.

The Three Legged Dog

A three legged dog wandered into Dodge City, Kansas, several years ago. One of his front legs was missing. Well, a three legged dog might not normally attract too much attention, but this dog was walking on his two good hind legs and wearing a set of matched six-shooters.

People really began to pay attention when the dog walked into the local saloon, shouldered up to the bar and barked:

"I'm looking for the

man who shot my paw!"

Prisoner's Proposition

Two inmates of the state prison in Canon City, Colorado, were due for parole. One day, out in the exercise yard, they were talking about what they planned to do after their sentences were finished.

One said to the other, "As soon as we get out we'll need money. I have a proposition. I know a small bank in Salida that will be a pushover."

During their exercise periods over the next several days they made detailed plans about how they would rob the bank. You can imagine their surprise when they went before the board to find their impending parole had been denied. Someone had overheard them and reported them to the warden.

This just goes to show again:

You should never end a sentence with a proposition!

Adages & Proverbs

Noah and the Adders

Y ou are all familiar with the story of Noah and the Ark.

There's a little-known side-light to the story. When the ark came to rest on Mount Ararat, Noah released two of each species.

"Go forth and multiply to replenish the earth," he told them.

In time Noah noticed that the only pair not mating and multiplying was a pair of snakes, the adders.

He said to God, "What should I do?"

God said, "Go get some lodge-pole pine trees. Cut them into pieces about 4 feet long, dig holes, and place them on the four corners of a square. Then put the adders in the middle of the square."

Noah followed God's instructions but there was no change in the behavior of the adders.

"What did I do wrong, God?" Noah asked.

"Oh, I forgot. Cut more logs, split them, and make a table, then place the adders on the table," God instructed.

Noah did as told and soon the adders began to reproduce.

"What difference did the raised table make?" Noah asked.

God replied:

"Any fool knows that adders can multiply on a log table!"

Honda Gas

J oe was a teacher who developed a health problem that made life quite difficult. Something occurred in his lower gastrointestinal tract that turned everything he ate to gas.

He hadn't yet turned 50, so the problem wasn't simply, as the comedian Bill Cosby was reported to have said, "After you turn 50, everything you eat turns to gas."

It became so bad that Joe had to occasionally walk out into the hallway during class to pass some gas or be embarrassed in front of the students. Eventually, his problem became so acute that, whenever he passed gas, it erupted so vigorously it sounded as though he was saying, "HONDA", from the rear. His strategy of unobtrusively stepping out into the hallway obviously wouldn't work anymore.

It was time to go see a doctor for some help. The doctor gave him a thorough examination, including a complete lower G.I.   During the consultation after the physical, he said, "You need to go see an eye, ear, nose and throat specialist."

Joe was flabbergasted and questioned the doctor's sanity.

The doctor said, "You'll understand after your appointment."

An appointment was arranged with a local throat specialist. She examined him carefully, then exclaimed, "Just as we suspected, you have an abscessed tooth."

Joe asked incredulously, "What possibly can an abscessed tooth have to do with flatulence?"

She replied:

"Everyone knows that absesses make the

farts go HONDA!"

The Indian Triangle

An Indian chief had three wives. He kept them in separate tepees to keep them happy. In addition, he provided each with a special sleeping arrangement.

One wife slept on a buffalo hide.

The second wife had a bear rug.

The third wife had a hippopotamus hide on the floor of her tepee.

As might be expected, it came to pass that each of the three wives became pregnant. The first wife had a bouncing baby girl, the second, a baby boy, and the third wife had twin boys.

This just goes to show again that:

The sum of the squaws on the two hides is equal to the squaw on the hippopotamus.

Pantomime

A number of years ago, Marcel Marceau, the famous French pantomime, took his show to Africa. While there he was taken on a river tour into a lush jungle area which was inhabited by a tribe of cannibals. Neither he nor his guide was ever seen again. Of course, when Marcel didn't return, the world of the stage was shocked by his disappearance. Help poured into the country from all over Europe. The best safari trackers were hired to find what had happened to him. After days of searching, one of the trackers found a single white glove under a banyan tree deep in the jungle. The glove was quickly identified as one worn by Mr. Marceau in his stage performances.

The searchers found several scantily clad natives hunting in the area where the glove had been found, but were unable to communicate with them in their native tongue. After several hours, a translator was found who agreed to interrogate the natives. When questioned about their dietary preferences, it became obvious that the natives were cannibals. The worst was feared for poor Marcel.

The native warriors became very excited when shown the white glove. After more questioning it was found they were excited and pleased because Marcel had been a particularly tasty morsel.

Even though the searchers were grieved to learn the fate of Marcel, they were much relieved to know of the pleasure he had brought to the cannibals because, as everyone knows:

A mime is a terrible thing to waste!

The Tea of Mercy

A number of years ago a rather hardy tourist who had been out roughing it in the bush country of Australia for weeks decided he needed to revisit civilization. He drove into a small bush town called Mercy where he found a small hotel, checked in and soaked the accumulated dirt off in a nice, long, bath. Then he went down to the lobby and asked the hotel clerk where he might find a restaurant.

The clerk recommended a place just down the street.

"You really ought to try the tea there. It is famous all over the territory. Its called Koala Tea," the clerk said.

The traveler walked to the restaurant, found a table and asked for a menu. Sure enough, prominently displayed at the top of the menu was an advertisement for Koala Tea. He ordered a cup to sip while he studied the menu.

When the tea came, he looked into the cup. The bottom was covered with sediment. There were also little bits and pieces of something floating around in the liquid.

He called the waitress over and said, "Miss, there must be something wrong with this tea. What are all these floating things in the cup?"

She replied, "Didn't you know?

The Koala Tea of Mercy

is not strained!"

Shakespeare's Bees

John the beekeeper was rather sadistic. He made life miserable for everyone around him with his mean tricks. Once, after watching the worker bees leave for the day's toil, he blocked the normal opening to the hive and painted a black arch on the opposite side to simulate the doorway.

He then sat nearby to watch as the bees returned laden with nectar. They would fly directly into the painted black arch, bang into the wood, and fall senseless to the ground below.

Two old bees were perched on the rim of the hive. One turned to the other and said:

"What bees these mortals fool!"

Benny and His Beard

Benny was down on his luck. Nothing seemed to be going right. He had lost his job; he had no money; he was developing an ulcer. But Benny maintained his religious faith and in his daily prayers he asked for something better. One day while he was praying, a voice came down from the heavens.

"Benny," said the voice, "I can help you. Your luck will change if you will promise not to shave. But if you fail to keep your promise I will immediately turn you into an urn."

Benny thought a bit, and said, "A beard can't be that bad. Sure, I promise not to shave."

The very next day Benny met a beautiful young lady, they fell in love and were soon married. Benny got a job with the company owned by his father-in-law. His health improved, he prospered and in time he fathered two lovely children. All things considered, they were a happy family.

However, after a few years, Benny's wife began to complain about his long beard. Benny didn't think much about it until one day, while walking down the street, he tripped over his beard.

"I'm going home to shave off this wretched beard right now," he said to himself.

When he arrived home, he marched into the bathroom, got out his razor and prepared to shave off the beard.

Then he heard the heavenly voice again, "Benny, are you sure you want to do that? Remember your promise!"

Benny thought a bit, and decided he might be able to wait a while longer. Months later the beard had grown so long he had to roll it up to keep from stepping on it. One morning while walking down some stairs, the beard unrolled, Benny got all tangled up in it and fell down the steps. Angered, he went back upstairs to the bathroom, got out his razor and started shaving.

The voice from above said, "I warned you what would happen, Benny!"

A bolt of lightning struck Benny, changing him into an urn. This just goes to prove again that:

A Benny shaved is a Benny urned!

Maxims

The Kurds and Yerms

Once upon a time, about 4000 years ago, a great army of Kurds (from Kurdistan in Iraq) swept across the Middle East, conquering vast areas of land. They pushed westward until they reached what is the present state of Israel. There, they met staunch resistance from a small tribe of mountain dwellers called the Yerms.

The Yerms were wonderful archers. They would simply wait in the hills until the Kurds passed through the valleys below. They would then shower the Kurdish soldiers with hundreds of arrows. For defense, the Yerms built a series of underground tunnels in which they could seek refuge whenever they were threatened.

After a long struggle, the Yerms were finally defeated, and the Kurds conquered Israel. There was one Yerm, however, who had not given up. He decided to exact revenge.

The Kurdish King had set up his capitol in Jerusalem, a city dominated by hills on the East. Through these hills there was only one narrow pass providing easy passage to Kurdistan. The last remaining Yerm guarded the pass and shot everyone who tried to get through. When the Kurdish soldiers came after him, he simply scuttled to safety in one of the tunnels the Yerms had dug.

This distressed the king of the Kurds. Because of one lowly Yerm, no important messages or emissaries could pass through from his kingdoms in the East.

Thinking it would take a small, scrawny soldier to follow the Yerm into the tunnels the king had his military leaders identify the scrawniest, fastest soldier in the army. He called the man to his throne room one day and told him to go into the hills alone at night, sneak into the Yerm's tunnels and capture that one last remaining Yerm. The soldier went out that very night but never returned.

The king then identified and commissioned his second scrawniest soldier to attempt the same thing. That second scrawny soldier was never seen again. For weeks, the King kept sending out his dwindling supply of scrawny soldiers but none ever returned.

The king had become terribly discouraged when, one day, a big, burly soldier appeared before him and claimed he could capture the Yerm. The king doubted the wisdom of the move but in his desperation he directed the burly Kurd to find and capture the wily Yerm.

The next morning, bright and early, the king was awakened by the return of the soldier who marched into the palace with the Yerm slung over his shoulder. The delighted king promptly promoted the Kurd to captain of the guard, and, as was Kurdish custom, made the Yerm his personal man-servant.

As the captain turned to leave, the king stopped him and asked, "Captain, how did you capture the Yerm?"

The big, burly soldier responded:

"Sire, everyone knows the burly Kurd catches the Yerm!"

A Sari Tale

Many years ago in India, a stick and a stone were of some small service to a Hindu holy man in a small village. Out of gratitude he offered to transform them into any object they desired.

The solid stone wanted to be a strongbox or safe to hold the holy man's sacred relics. The vain stick indicated it wanted to become a Hindu woman's beautiful gown or sari. It thus came to pass; the stone became a strongbox and the stick became a sari.

The night of the transformation, a terrible fire ravaged the village, burning down every house. The holy man's hut was destroyed and along with it the beautiful sari. The safe was the only thing that survived.

This just proves again:

It's better to be safe than sari!

Grass Huts

O n a beautiful south sea island, there once lived a king whose proudest possession was his peacock throne. Most days, in his seashore village, he spent his free time polishing and cleaning the throne.

One day the head medicine man came to the king with a warning. "A huge typhoon is coming. We must move to high ground!"

"I can't leave my throne. It might get wet. You go with all the others to high ground. I'll stay here," said the king.

The medicine man said, "You can't possibly stay. You will be killed. The wind and waves will be too strong to endure."

After a long and heated conference, the king's advisors convinced him that the throne would be safe if they stowed it in the rafters of the grass hut where the king lived. After stowing the throne in the rafters and took off for the hills.

Sure enough, the typhoon came. The waters rose higher and the wind blew harder than expected. When the storm abated, the villagers returned to the village. Everything had been washed away, including the king's hut and throne.

This proves, without a doubt:

People who live in grass huts shouldn't stow thrones!

The Doctor and the Well

A middle aged doctor was becoming burned out. One day he didn't go into the office but chose to stay on his farm. Most of the day, he sat on the edge of the well dropping pebbles into the water below. About mid-afternoon, his nurse drove out to the farm to ask that he come to the office because they had so many patients there.

He said, "I'll come soon, my dear."

About an hour later, when he had not come to the office, his nurse returned. As she drove up, he turned toward her, slipped and fell into the well and drowned.

The moral of this story is:

Doctors should treat the sick and leave the well alone!

The Painted Church

In one of the New England states, a small Protestant parish occupied a beautiful old clapboard church. Through the years the church had weathered badly, so was in need of new paint. It was a poor church so the parishioners didn't have the money to have the building painted by professionals.

They decided to take up a collection to purchase the paint then have volunteers do the job. The paint was purchased and one Saturday the job was started by a happy crew.

When the volunteers were about half finished painting the building, they recognized that they were going to be short of paint. They stopped to talk over their problem. After their discussion, it became obvious there was no way they could expect more donations to buy more paint.

It was decided the only thing to do was to thin what paint remained and continue the job. When they were finished with everything except the steeple, they again realized they were running short of paint. They did the only thing possible- they thinned what little paint remained and finished the job.

No sooner had they finished than a huge thundercloud came scudding overhead. Lightning flashed, thunder roared, and it rained buckets. All the thinned paint was washed off their beloved church building.

As the storm ended, a thunderous voice was heard from on high. The voice cried:

"Repaint, repaint,

and thin No More!"

Chicken Counts

There once was a king who learned of a plot against his throne. He concluded, after a lengthy investigation, that a group of counts were hatching a plot against him.

He had one of the counts thrown into irons, dragged before him and demanded to be told the truth about the conspirators.

The count said, "I'll never tell! I'll never tell no matter what you do to me!"

The King called in the executioner. The count's head was placed on the block. Just as the King gave the signal, the count had a change of heart.

He cried out, "Wait, wait, I'll tell!"

But it was too late. The executioner could not stop his motion! Down came the axe and off came the head. The King never learned who the other plotters were.

All of which goes to show:

One shouldn't hatchet one's counts before they chicken!

King Ozymandias

King Ozymandias of Assyria was running low on cash after years of war with the Hittites. His last great possession was the Star of the Euphrates, the most valuable diamond in the ancient world. Desperate, he went to Croesus, the pawnbroker, to ask for a loan.

Croesus said, "I'll give you 100,000 dinars for it."

"But I paid a million dinars for it," the King protested. "Don't you know who I am? I am the king!"

Croesus replied:

"When you wish to pawn a star, it makes no difference who you are."

Gastronomical

British Turncoats

During the Revolutionary War there was a lone British soldier who became isolated from his brigade. He took shelter in the chicken house on a farm near Boston. He hid out there for several days without being apprehended.

While hiding there one night, he heard the thunder of hooves approaching. He looked out and saw a man on horseback riding past. He recognized the man as the intrepid Paul Revere riding through the night to warn of the impending British attack.

The tory soldier knew what he had to do. He took careful aim, preparing to shoot Paul in the back, but a chicken attacked him just as he was ready to fire. Because of the cackling and commotion, he was captured.

Since then a statue has been built on the spot to commemorate:

The first chicken to catch a Tory!

South American Constipation

An anthropologist traveled to South America searching for local herbal medicines. He spent months traveling up and down the Amazon River visiting local tribes. In each village he collected information and samples to take back home.

In one village he was shown a fern, the leaves of which were reported to be a sure cure for constipation. The anthropologist, being somewhat skeptical, questioned the local tribal chief in great detail about how the potion made from the fern was to be prepared and administered. When the anthropologist still expressed his doubts, the chief looked him in the eye and said:

"Trust me... with fronds like these, you don't need enemas."

Joe Torre

J oe Torre, former manager of the Atlanta Braves baseball team, used to catch for the New York Mets. In one game, with the bases loaded, the batter hit a long fly ball to center field. The man on third base tagged up and ran for home. The center fielder caught the ball and threw directly to home plate. The throw was right on target and in plenty of time but Joe, the catcher, stepped aside as the runner came sliding into the plate with spikes held high. The runner was safe!

Casey Stengel, the Mets manager, charged out of the dugout, stood face-to-face with Joe and yelled:

"*What's the matter with you, chicken catcher Torre?*"

Snails and Rabbits

A snail who struck it rich in the oil business decided he needed a faster way to get around. Tired of going at a snail's pace, he decided to buy a small car. After looking at advertisements in the local paper, he decided a Volkswagen would be most appropriate for a snail so he went to the local VW dealer. He looked at the various models and chose a VW Rabbit. While crawling around the car he noticed the chrome rabbit emblem on the back.

"That's not a suitable symbol for a snail," he said to himself.

"Can you remove that chrome rabbit emblem?" he asked the dealer.

"Certainly, but it will leave two holes that we'll have to cover up," the dealer replied.

"Could you get a chrome capital S to replace the rabbit?" the snail asked.

"Sure," the dealer said. "It'll take a few days though. Can you wait?"

"I'm in no hurry," said the snail.

The snail came back in three days to pick up his new car. As he drove out of the parking lot, two old ladies standing on the sidewalk noticed the snail in his car.

One turned to the other and said:

"Did you see that

escargot?"

Artie

rtie was a hit man. Artie was very ingenious. He didn't always use a gun to do in his marks. He was adept with a stiletto, the garrote, whatever was best for a particular target.

His best friend, George, was the produce manager at the local Safeway supermarket. One Friday, at their weekly T.G.I.F. meeting at the local bar, they started complaining about their pet peeves. George despised the ladies who came into the produce section at Safeway and fondled the fruit.

Over the years his anger had festered and grown all out of proportion. He explained to Artie that he could barely stand it some days. One little old lady in particular had been getting on his nerves the past few weeks. She came in almost every morning about the same time and walked up and down the aisles in the produce department fondling the fruit.

Artie said, "You're really in bad shape. Is there anything I could do to help?"

"There's no way I could afford to pay your fee, Artie," replied George.

"You're my best friend, George. What could you pay?"

After rummaging through his pockets George said, "I'm almost broke, Artie. This is all the money I have to my name."

He placed his entire worldly possessions on the bar between them. There was one dollar bill and a small assortment of coins. They counted them out and found it came to $1.49.

Artie said, "The money isn't that important. I'll do in the lady just for you. How do I recognize her and what time does she usually come into the store?"

After thinking a while, George said, "You'll have no trouble at all. She is a little old lady with white hair and wears a long black coat and old, dirty, tennis shoes. She comes in every Monday morning about 9:00 o'clock."

On Monday morning Artie arrived at the Safeway early and hung around the produce department. About 8:45 a little old lady with white hair and a long black coat came down the fruit aisle stopping at each bin to examine the fruit. Artie decided she must be his fruit fondler. He sneaked up behind her, slipped a short piece of rope around her neck, and strangled her. It was quick and quiet. As she fell to the floor he noticed she was wearing brown loafers.

As he was hurrying out the front door of Safeway, he met a second small white-haired old lady wearing a black coat who did have on dirty, white tennis shoes. He decided to be sure he got the right lady so strangled her, too.

In the parking lot he bumped into a third little old white-haired lady wearing a long black coat and dirty white tennis shoes. By this time he was rattled. He decided quickly to be absolutely sure that George's problem was solved, so he strangled her, too.

All of this had taken several minutes. The first lady had been found and the police called immediately. They apprehended Artie while he was taking care of the third lady.

The headline in the newspaper the next day read:

Artie chokes three for $1.49 at Safeway!

Musical

The Martians

When we sent our first expedition to Mars, members of the landing crew were surprised to find the planet inhabited. On their first expedition away from the spaceship, after miles of driving across the desert-like terrain, three little furry creatures popped up from behind some boulders. They took the astronauts captive, marched them into a cave and locked them in a cell.

Hours later, when the three little furry fellows came back, the astronauts demanded, "Take us to your leader."

The little furry fellows seemed to understand because they unlocked the door and marched the astronauts down a long hall. A door at the end of the hall opened into a huge room. There, sitting on a throne, was another furry creature, but he was different from the others. He had what appeared to be a hypodermic needle sticking out of the top of his head.

One of the astronauts exclaimed, "Who are you?"

He replied:

"I'm the furry with the syringe on top!"

"The Surrey with the Fringe on Top"

The Silent Monks

There is a monastery near Aspen, Colorado, called Snowmass. All the monks living there have taken a vow of silence. They rarely speak. Each day begins with morning vespers.

The service starts when the head abbot comes in and chants, "Good morning."

The monks chant in reply, "Good morning."

They don't say another word until evening vespers, when the head abbot comes in and chants, "Good evening."

The monks all reply in unison, "Good evening." Not another word is spoken until the next morning.

Several years ago one of the monks decided he had to break up the boredom of this routine.

The next morning when the head abbot chanted, "Good morning," all the other monks responded, "Good morning."

Except the one bored monk who chanted, "Good evening."

Quickly, the head abbot chanted in reply:

"Some one chanted evening."

Beethoven

Several years ago, a friend and I were driving along the Danube River in Austria. We noticed what seemed to be a cave entrance down near the water line. Since we were both confirmed spelunkers, we grabbed our ropes, lights and other gear, and went down for a look around.

We crawled through the opening and discovered a huge cavern. Our explorations took us into the farthest reaches of the cavern where we came upon what appeared to be a dusty old box. We scraped some of the dust off and found an inscription, "Beethoven."

My friend insisted that we open the box. He pried of the top. When we shined our lights into the box, we saw a skeleton with a rubber eraser in one hand and a sheet of music in the other.

Sure enough, it was Beethoven:

decomposing.

Roy Rogers & Trigger

Some of you may not be old enough to remember Roy Rogers. He was a famous cowboy movie star during the '1940s and '50s.

What was his famous horse's name?

That's right, Trigger.

And the name of Roy's wife?

DaleEvans, remember?

One day when Roy was on the set shooting a movie, he got a call from Dale to hurry home. He jumped into his pickup truck in full costume; alligator boots, star spangled shirt and sequined pants.

As he drove into the ranch yard
Dale was waiting for him on the
front porch.

"A mountain lion has killed all
the chickens," Dale cried. "You'll
have to do something."

Being a man of action Roy
saddled up Trigger, put his
carbine in the scabbard and rode
off looking for the big cat. As he
was riding along the trail, the cat
jumped him from a tree. Roy was
knocked from the saddle with the
cat ripping and tearing at him as
they fell to the ground. With his
usual superhuman effort, Roy was
able to tear himself free, grab his
rifle and shoot the mountain lion.
He was a mess! His shirt was torn
and tattered. Many of the sequins

were ripped off his pants. His alligator boots had been ripped and chewed.

Roy threw the carcass of the cat behind the saddle, mounted and rode back to the ranch house. Dale came running to meet him, singing:

Pardon me, Roy, is that the cat that chewed your new shoes?"

"Chattanooga Choo Choo"

Freud

B ack around the turn of the century in Vienna, a lady developed a psychological problem. She couldn't talk at all. She needed help!

She did what everyone did before the advent of the internet. She went directly to the yellow pages of the local telephone book. She checked the listings and settled on a newly listed psychiatrist, Sigmund Freud. Since she couldn't talk she had a friend make an appointment for her to undergo psychoanalysis.

Her treatment was peculiar because she couldn't talk. Each session she simply lay on the couch for the allotted hour, and Freud would mutter a few words just before she left. It didn't appear as if they were making any progress at all.

Then came a day when she lay on the couch and chattered away without stopping. Freud couldn't get a word in edgewise. When the hour was over, she rose from the couch and danced around the room singing:

"Pardon me, Freud, does this chatter mean I'm cuckoo?"

The Shadow

Prior to the time television arrived many people gathered around their radios in the evening to listen to serials. One of those serials was, "The Shadow." The show always began with the sound of a creaking door opening accompanied by the phrase, "Who knows what evil lurks in the hearts of men? The *SHADOW* knows." The Shadow's sidekick was named Roy.

Once, as a reward for a case well-solved, the Shadow received a box of his favorite candies. He just loved chocolate covered nougats. The Shadow, knowing that Roy also loved chocolates, hid the box in the bottom drawer of his dresser.

The following day when the Shadow was away on a case alone, after a long search, Roy found the box of chocolate nougats. He had just taken his first succulent bite of one of the chocolates when he heard the Shadow come in the front door.

He quickly replaced the half-eaten nougat just as the Shadow came into the room. The Shadow opened the box, saw the half-eaten chocolate and sang:

"Pardon me, Roy, is that the Shadow's

nougat you chewed?"

Chess

One weekend, my wife and I went down to the Brown Palace Hotel in Denver to watch the chess tournament. The players were all seated at tables in the two-story foyer near the entrance.

After wandering around for some time, we noticed two men back in a corner arguing vigorously. We sidled over to eavesdrop a bit. It turned out they were arguing about who was the best chess player.

The argument went on interminably. We finally left because we got tired listening to:

Chess nuts boasting in an open foyer.

Think of *"The Christmas Song."*

Red Sons

An Indian chief, who became wealthy after oil was discovered on his reservation, decided to send his two sons to college so the tribe would have good leadership after he was gone.

One son went to Harvard and the other to Yale. Both did well and in due time entered law school. Much to the disappointment of their father, when they received their degrees they decided not to return to the reservation. Eventually both settled in San Francisco to practice law.

They were very successful and soon became wealthy. Among other things, both bought sailboats and became members of an exclusive yacht club. The old chief soon overcame his previous disappointment because he achieved fame as the father of the:

Red sons in the sail set.

Recall the old song *Red Sails in the Sunset.*

Sam Frank

Harry and Sam Frank were identical twins. Their mother raised them accordingly. She dressed them in matching clothes, combed their hair the same way, fed them the same food and even gave them identical gifts. As they grew, they went to the same elementary and secondary schools. They were identical in every respect from infancy to young manhood. Then, after graduating from college, they went separate ways.

Harry married a fine, upstanding girl, raised a healthy family of three, went to church every Sunday, and was a pillar of the community.

Sam, on the other hand, was led astray by a wanton who steered him into a life of debauchery.

It may have been coincidence but the twins died nearly the same time. When they approached the pearly gates, Sam was sent to hell but

Harry was welcomed to heaven. Sam was adaptable; he had no trouble making a home in hell. Sizing up the situation, he opened a disco night club which was very successful. The clientele living in hell loved to dance, among other things.

Sam did very well until one night he lost the string player in his combo. Being resourceful, he called up Harry in heaven to ask if he would come down to play the harp for just one night. Harry sought permission from Saint Peter.

"You can do it if you will abide by one condition. You must be back in heaven before the sun rises," Saint Peter said.

Harry agreed without hesitation. He packed up his harp and went down to hell. Sam's disco was jammed with people dancing and partying.

Time passed quickly and soon it was 5:00 o'clock in the morning. Harry was having so much fun that he had forgotten the time. Just as the sun began to rise he remembered his promise to Saint Peter.

"I've got to get back," he told Sam. "Saint Pete will really be mad if I'm late." He dashed back up to heaven as fast as he could.

As he entered the gates, Saint Peter stopped him and asked, "Harry, where is your harp?"

He answered, "Oh,

I left my harp

in Sam Frank's disco!"

"I Left My Heart in San Francisco"

Strange Daiquiris

A small town doctor had been going into the local bar every day after work for years to have a daiquiri before going home to his wife and dinner. He had come to like a rather special daiquiri, made with walnuts. It had become such a regular habit that whenever the bartender saw the doctor approaching his bar he automatically started making a walnut daiquiri.

One day in mid-afternoon the bartender was checking his supplies and found he had no walnuts. There wasn't time before the doctor arrived to run to the store to get more. The bartender rummaged around and found a few hickory nuts.

"If I grind these up and put them in the walnut jar, the doc will never know," he thought. He had just finished when the doctor walked in for his daily libation. The bartender casually mixed the drink and served the doctor. After the first sip, the doctor asked, "What is this?"

The bartender replied: "That's a:

hickory daiquiri, Doc!"

Oppornockity

S everal years ago in a large city in the western United States, a lady inherited a large grand piano. The piano had been the prize possession of the lady's favorite aunt. She arranged for the piano to be moved across town and up the three flights of stairs to her apartment by a professional piano moving company. They accomplished the task with the utmost care, but, when she sat down to play the instrument, she found it to be badly out of tune.

She, of course, was not going to call just any piano tuner so she abstained from playing the piano for several days while she inquired from her many music-loving friends as to the best piano tuner in the city. Several people she questioned referred her to Mr. Oppornockity. She called and found that he was a very busy and expensive man, but finally arranged for a piano tuning date two weeks in the future.

On the morning Mr. Oppornockity was to arrive, she had arranged to be late for work so she could meet him in her apartment. When he arrived she found him to be a very disagreeable old fellow. He was almost blind, hard of hearing, and very curt and blunt in his comments. He complained about the placement of the piano in the room, the polish she had used on the wood and the general condition of the instrument. Even though she did her best to mollify him, he would not allow her to leave for her office without paying him for the work ahead of time. Reluctantly, she paid him, and hurried off.

After a day at the office, during which she accomplished very little because of her concern with her prize piano, five o'clock finally inched around and she headed straight home. The first thing she did after throwing her coat onto a chair in the corner was sit down to play a few bars on the piano. To her dismay the sound from the strings was no better than it had been when she first tried out the instrument several days before. She immediately went to the telephone to complain. After she had explained the problem in great detail she was startled to hear:

"Oppornockity tunes

but once!"

Beethoven's Ninth

The symphony orchestra was performing Beethoven's Ninth symphony before a sparse audience. As those of you who love classical music are probably aware, in the piece, there is a long passage in one of the movements, lasting about 20 minutes, during which the bass violists have nothing to do.

Rather than sit around that whole time with nothing to do, one night the bassists decided to sneak offstage and go to the tavern next door for a quick one.

After slamming several beers in quick succession, one of them looked at his watch and said, "Hey! We need to get back!"

"There's no need to panic," said a fellow bassist. "I thought we might need some extra time, so I tied the last few pages of the conductor's score together with string. It'll take him a few minutes to get it untangled."

A few moments later they staggered back to the concert hall and took their places in the orchestra. About this time, a member of the audience noticed the conductor was frantically struggling with his score and said as much to her companion.

"Well, of course," said her companion:

*"Don't you see?
It's the bottom of the
Ninth, the score
is tied,
and the bassists are
loaded!"*

Advertising Slogans

Hugh and the Flowers

E ven back in the middle ages occasionally priests left the fold to pursue worldly goals. One mendicant friar, tired of begging, turned to the florist trade. He thought he could earn a living selling flowers to the people of his home village. He quickly learned the people were so poor they could hardly buy food, let alone his flowers.

Depressed and angered by his failure, the friar became a deranged people-hater who offered poisoned flowers to the passing villagers. Any poor soul who smelled the flowers promptly fell over dead.

Outraged, the village council sent the sheriff to arrest the friar. But the sheriff foolishly accepted a flower from the friar, took a whiff of its fragrance and fell over dead. Then the council deputized the fire marshal to arrest the deranged friar. The results were the same-one dead fireman. The members of council were beside themselves. How could the mad florist be apprehended? No one wanted to risk his or her life.

Finally, little four-foot-six Hugh stepped forward.

"I'm not afraid to manacle the mad monk," he said.

Everyone was astonished at his bravery. After the council had deputized Hugh, he marched off on his mission. When the demented friar offered Hugh a flower, he refused it. The deflated friar then meekly submitted to arrest and Hugh took him off to jail.

This proves once again that:

Only Hugh can prevent florist friars!

Sesame Street Bus

A new driver was hired for the Sesame Street bus. After the usual training period, the big day arrived for his first run.

He started out early in the morning. At the first stop, he saw a huge fat lady waiting on the bench. She was so obese he didn't think she could get through the door of the bus.

But she squeezed her way aboard and, as she paid the fare, said, "Hi, my name is Patty. You're a new driver, aren't you?"

He said, "Yes I am. Take a seat so we can go."

At the second stop, he found another huge lady waiting.

She wiggled her way onto the bus, paid her money and said, "Hi, my name is Patty."

The driver said, "We already have one Patty on board."

Patty replied, "Yes, we both ride this bus every day."

At the third stop a little pip-squeak of a fellow leaped up on the steps of the bus, paid his money and said, "Hi, my name is Lester. You're a new driver, aren't you?"

The driver said, "Yes, please hurry, we're running late."

Lester walked to the back of the bus. The driver noticed in his rear view mirror that Lester took off a shoe and started paring the bunions on his foot with a pocket knife.

The driver thought to himself; "My gosh, that's weird."

He drove on and at the next stop a great big husky fellow dashed through the door and said gruffly, "My name is Ross. Some folks call me 'Special Ross'."

Then Ross walked back to sit with Lester. The driver saw Ross pull out a deck of cards. As he watched in his mirror he noticed that Ross was cheating.

At the last stop, a well dressed fellow started to pay his fare as he got on the bus, but after looking at the other passengers, he stopped and said:

"No, I'll not ride this bus with two obese Pattys,

Special Ross, cheating, Lester, picking bunions, on a Sesame Street bus."

McDonald restaurants old advertising slogan was, "Two all beef patties, special sauce, cheese, lettuce, pickles and onions on a sesame seed bun."

Cheeks of Tan

A Chinese woodcarver named Tan became famous carving statues called cheeks. One day a rather unique bear came by to watch Tan carve. He was a perfectly normal bear except that his feet were not bear feet. They left footprints like the feet of a little boy.

After watching Tan for a long time the bear picked up a statue and ran off into the woods.

One of Tan's helpers ran after him calling:

"*Come back, boy foot bear with cheeks of Tan.*"

The Goldberg Brothers

Here's a little factoid that might be of interest to automotive buffs. The four Goldberg brothers, Lowell, Norman, Hiram, and Max, invented and developed the first automobile air-conditioner.

On July 17, 1946, the temperature in Detroit was 97 degrees. The four brothers walked into old man Henry Ford's office and sweet-talked his secretary into telling him that four gentlemen were there with the most exciting innovation in the auto industry since the electric starter. Henry was curious and invited them into his office.

They refused and instead asked that he come out to the parking lot to their car. They persuaded him to get into the car, which was about 130 degrees because it had been sitting in the sun for some time. They then turned on the air conditioner and had soon cooled the interior to a comfortable temperature.

Mr. Ford got very excited and invited them back to the office, where he offered them $3 million for the patent. The brothers refused, saying they would settle for $2 million, but they wanted the recognition by having a label, "The Goldberg Air Conditioner" on the dashboard of each car in which it was installed.

Now old man Ford was more than just a little anti-Semitic, and there was no way he was going to put the Goldberg's name on several million Fords.

They haggled back and forth for about two hours and finally agreed on $4 million with the provision that just their first names would be shown on each auto dashboard.

So, to this day, all Ford air conditioners show:

Lo, Norm, Hi, and Max on the air conditioner controls.

Kermit the Frog

Kermit the frog went into the local savings and loan association to apply for a loan.

When he explained what he wanted to the lady at the counter, she replied, "You'll have to talk to Patty Wack, our chief loan officer."

Kermit said, "OK, where do I find her?"

The clerk pointed to a desk across the room where a pretty young lady was sitting.

He walked over to her and said, "I'm Kermit the frog. I need a loan."

"We'll be glad to help," she replied. "But of course, we'll need collateral. What do you have of value?"

"I don't have much of value, but I do have a nice statuette of Miss Piggy," Kermit told her.

Patty Wack said, "I'm afraid that will never do."

Kermit said, "But it's really a valuable statue."

"Go get the statue, so I can see it," said Patty Wack.

Kermit ran home for the statue and returned with it for Patty Wack to examine.

Patty Wack carefully looked it over and said, "No, I don't think this will do. But let me check with the president of the association to see what he thinks."

She took the Miss Piggy statue to the office of the president. He carefully looked it over, and said:

"That's a nice knick-knack, Patty Wack.

Give the frog a loan."

Japanese Names

A Japanese car manufacturer had designed a new model but could not come up with an appropriate name for it. Names are very important to the Japanese. For example ATOYOTA is spelled the same forward and backward.

Believing the Germans had chosen well when they named the Volkswagen (the people's car) the Japanese firm sent a delegation to the Volkswagen plant in Wolfsburg, Germany, to ask for help.

The VW president found that his people who invented model names were too busy to respond quickly. He asked the Japanese how soon they needed the new name.

When they replied that the car was almost ready for production and they needed a name as soon as possible, the German exclaimed:

"dat soon!!!"

Mel Famey

Mel Famey was a nationally famous baseball pitcher, a 20-game winner for several seasons with the Chicago Black Socks. One particularly good year, because of Mel's outstanding pitching, they went to the World Series.

In the series, Mel pitched the first game and, of course, the Black Socks won easily. After a rest of only two days, Mel was called upon to pitch the fourth series game. The Black Socks again won handily.

The other team, the New York Yankees, then won two games and tied the series at three games apiece.

Naturally the manager of the Black Socks picked Mel to pitch the seventh and deciding game. He had a no-hit, no-run game through the sixth inning and the Black Socks were ahead 1-0. The Yankees' manager, desperately trying to figure out a way to get to Famey, called a team meeting in the dugout. Someone pointed out that Mel really liked beer. The Yankees decided to slip a six-pack of beer into the Black Socks dugout where Mel would find it. Quickly, the job was done. Mel found the six-pack and downed two beers while his team was batting in the seventh inning.

In the eighth inning, Mel's pitching began to get a little erratic but he held the Yankees at bay. He then finished off the remaining four beers in the six-pack between the eighth and ninth innings.

In the ninth inning, he was a little wild. The Yankees got several hits and tied the score. With the bases loaded, Mel walked in the winning run. After the game, all the sports writers had the same question when they interviewed the team managers.

"What happened to Mel Famey?"

The Yankee manager ran into the Black Socks dugout and found the empty six-pack of beer. When he came out holding the empty carton high, he cried:

"This is the beer that made Mel Famey walk us!"

(The Stroh Brewery Company was the producer of Old Milwaukee beer whose advertising slogan provides the basis for this parody.)

The Pier

Two young men were out on a beach in California playing it cool, drinking beer and enjoying life. After several beers, they got into an argument about the length of the pier they could see from their spot on the beach.

One of them said, "I know exactly how far that pier extends out into the ocean. I helped build it several years ago."

"How long is it?" asked the other.

The first one said, "It's 144 feet long."

The other said, "No way, it can't possibly be 144 feet long! How do you know that?"

The man who had worked on the pier said, "We used exactly 216 planks and each one was eight inches wide. Figure it out: 216 times 8 divided by 12 is 144."

The other man continued to argue. Eventually, they decided the only way to settle the argument was to for one of them to count the planks on the pier.

The argumentative man agreed to crawl the length of the pier, counting the planks as he went. His friend, waiting on the beach, was astounded when he saw the crawler go right off the end of the pier and fall into the ocean.

When the man came staggering back, soaked to the skin, his friend asked, "What happened?"

"Well, I decided to ignore the planks and count the slits between them, but I forgot:

When your out of slits, you're out of pier!"

(Stroh Brewery Company was the producer of Schlitz beer, one of whose advertising slogan provided the basis for this parody.)

Molybdenum Sinks

Several years ago, Climax Molybdenum was having financial difficulties. Production cutbacks in the steel industry had reduced molybdenum sales seriously.

Climax put its researchers to work looking for new uses for molybdenum. They came up with an alloy they thought would be ideal for stainless steel sinks. Thousands were manufactured and sold.

Soon though, complaints began to inundate Climax; the sinks were turning brown. Back to work went the researchers. After weeks of effort they solved the problem.

Climax started making new sinks and assigned their marketing division to find a slogan to overcome the negative image left by the brown sinks. The advertising slogan that soon appeared in every paper across the land implored people to buy:

The unbrownable molly sinks!!!

The New Gnu

A number of years ago a problem developed at the San Diego Zoo. A new gnu was due but there wasn't room in the old gnu house for the new gnu. An addition was obviously needed for the gnu house.

The new gnu arrived before the new gnu house addition was completed. Since gnus just don't tolerate crowding, a special staff meeting was called to find a solution to the problem. The only work remaining to complete on the addition was to apply the tile on the floors and walls. The staff decided to pile part of the new tile down the middle of the room to contain the new gnu while they worked on the other half.

When the workers arrived the following day they were amazed to find the new gnu's half of the room was completely tiled. The workers were baffled. So was the staff. The new gnu was moved to the other side of the remaining tile pile until the mystery was solved. To everyone's amazement, when the workers again returned the next morning they found the whole new gnu house tiled floor to ceiling.

Another staff meeting was called. Then the board of directors held a special meeting. The directors decided to call in a consultant from New York. He spent three days at $500 per day studying the situation before producing this report:

"You have a typical gnu and a tiler, too!"

Traditional Shaggy Dog Story

The Race Horses

J ake and Lucky were Kentucky bred thoroughbred race horses. While young they led the proverbial "good life" for horses. They were free to frisk about in their assigned pasture to their hearts content, with all the sweet, luscious Kentucky blue grass to eat that any horse might desire.

Early in their training, it became obvious that Lucky was the faster of the two horses. Jake did his best but, except on those few days when Lucky was "off his feed," he just could not seem to come in with a faster time.

One day, when they were alone in the pasture, Lucky said to Jake, "Let's race around the field, Jake!"

Jake replied, "I don't want to race you, Lucky. You always win so why should I even try to race you?"

Lucky answered, "It's such a beautiful day and I feel so great, Jake, that I'll just take it easy so you can win. Please race with me."

Jake said, "O.K., Lucky, let's go!"

He took off with a whinny with Lucky in hot pursuit as they raced around the perimeter of the pasture. He led most of the way but near the finish, Lucky, with a burst of speed, pulled into the lead as they crossed the line.

After regaining their breath, Jake said, "You said you would take it easy and let me win, Lucky. Why didn't you keep your word?"

Lucky said, "I'm sorry, Jake, but in the heat of our race, I simply forgot. I'll not do it again."

Later that year, when the two horses were entered in their first race, Lucky won easily and Jake came in as an "also ran." Several weeks later, when they were again alone in their pasture, Lucky once again was feeling at his frisky best.

He said to Jake, "Let's race, Jake!"

Jake sulked off, head held low. Lucky stayed at his heels nibbling the sweet grass. With each succeeding bite of the savory grass Lucky's spirits rose.

Finally he couldn't stand more

and said, "Jake, if you will just run with me around the pasture, we don't have to call it a race. I'll run along behind you. You can cross the finish line first."

Jake thought a minute and said, "It's such a beautiful day, Lucky. I'll take your word. Let's go!"

Off they ran through the knee-deep grass with Jake in the lead and Lucky right on his heels. They whinnied with delight as they ran at full gallop. Near the end of the course, Jake began to tire. Lucky had stamina to spare and passed Jake with ease. He crossed the finish line a full length ahead of Jake. Needless to say, Jake was heartbroken. It was several days before he would even talk with Lucky. When they finally made up, Lucky apologized endlessly. Jake accepted grudgingly but vowed he would never race Lucky again.

Lucky went on to win almost every race in which he was entered: the Kentucky Derby, the Preakness, the Belmont Stakes. He had a long and illustrious career. Whenever he was not racing, he was often returned to the pasture with his best friend Jake. Jake delighted in hearing of Lucky's triumphs, but won very few races himself.

Years later, after both had been retired from racing, when they were standing in the shade of the barn, Lucky suggested to Jake that they should gallop around the pasture, just for old time's sake.

Jake replied, "You know I won't do that, Lucky, because you always win."

"On my word of honor, Jake, this time will be different," Lucky said. "I'll control myself and let you cross the finish line first."

Reluctantly, Jake said, "Don't run very fast, though. My old bones hurt too much when I gallop like we did years ago."

Lucky agreed and they trotted off around the field. When they had almost completed the circuit, Jake tired badly so he slowed to a walk. Lucky still had lots of energy so he cantered on ahead. He again finished in the lead as they neared the barn.

When they had both stopped near the barn, an old dog who had observed the unfolding saga for years said, "I could have told you, Jake. You should have known. Lucky can't be trusted. He will always win whenever he runs."

Jake turned to Lucky and said:

"Look, Lucky,

a talking dog!"

THE AUTHORS

GENE CHILD collected these "shaggy dog" stories with puns or other types of wordplay for punch lines during his 33-year teaching career in secondary schools in Kansas, Germany, Colorado, and Kenya. Physics was a difficult subject for many so he added some levity to his classes by telling these stories at the end of class every Friday. He feels that the creative use of humor in the classroom is essential for a well rounded education.

GENE YOUNGMANN has been painting transparent watercolors since 1981 along the Front Range Mountains west of Denver. His subjects of choice are Colorado landscapes, vintage automobiles and aging architecture. He is a retired high school art teacher, having taught drawing for twenty-five years at Golden High School in Golden, CO. During sometimes tedious faculty meetings he perfected his ability to do pencil sketches of those around him.

His web site is www.youngmannwatercolors.com.

When together they are sometimes known as

"A Pair of Genes".